AKWESASNE M
SOCIAL SONGS AND DANCES

Shatekaronhioton- Corey Fox
Tehoniehtaronweh- Donovan Thompson
Karahkwino-Tina Square

Book design and Cover art by
Kanietakeron- Dave Fadden

Edited by
Konwahahawi- Sarah Rourke

Mohawk Writing:
Karonhianonhna- JoAnn Swamp

Resources
from the Original Rotinonhshon:ni Ahwesahsne
Mohawk Social Dances book.

The Akwesasne Mohawk Social Dances CD pairs with this Social Dance book. The CD contains the songs that we sing at socials for learning purposes, sung by our male cultural educators Shatekaronhioton Fox and Donovan Thompson of the Native North American Travelling College. Produced by our Cultural A.V. technician Raienkonnis Edwards.

Produced for and by the Native North American Travelling College Copyright 2017

Social Dance

A social dance is a way for our Haudenosaunee people to gather with one another to dance and sing our traditional social songs. Social Dances are not ceremonial dances and they can be held anytime of the year. Socials are times when our people come together to share in laughter and friendship in an informal gathering. Whenever socials are held, it is important that all the people behave in the appropriate way. This means there is a zero tolerance on alcohol and drugs. We create a positive environment for elders and youth to share in their songs, dances and stories. It is also important that parents make sure their children are not running free and playing around. They are taught to respect the space and those who are hosting the event. Each song or speaker is a lesson for all who attend. We must sit and be observant to those teachings.

At the beginning of the social, a speaker will stand up to say the Ohen:ton Karihwatehkwen (the words that come before all else). This is recited to give thanks to all that has been given to us in creation. The people sit in silence and listen. They say "Tho" at the end of each section as a sign that they agree with the thanksgiving address. This is conducted at the beginning and the end of the social dance. The speaker will also stand up and announce who will sing and what song will be sung. This will notify all singers who would like to join, to get ready. They will grab their rattles and set up the benches in the middle of the room to accommodate participants in the song. People attending the social will listen to hear what dance is next and prepare. Depending on the upcoming dance, they may need a male/female partner or change their shoes to join in the fun.

Singing Society

A singing society is a group of men and/or women who create a group to sing for their communities. There are two or more groups that represent each nation of the Haudenosaunee Confederacy. However, singing is not their only responsibility. They represent their communities by the work they do to provide help or support for their nation. For example, a male singing group may stack or chop wood for the longhouse. Or the women's group may sing for a funeral service or community fundraiser. They are good role models for the community and spread joy to the different nations or communities through their music. Every six months, a "Sing" is held in order to bring all of the Haudenosaunee People together to socialize in unity and friendship. Each singing group will create a set of 5 songs of women's dance that they can share amongst the other nations. The duties of each singing group before the sing is to report to the Nation that is hosting the sing, what work they have done in their community. Each singing group must conduct themselves in a humble and respectable manner because they are representing their community. The sing will change venue with every event, so that each nation has an opportunity to be the host. This event is carried out every six months, once in the spring and once in the fall to continue the good work and good friendship with our whole confederacy.

Things that are needed to have a Social

People to visit and watch, a positive environment, good mind, a housekeeper, singers, dancers, a Mohawk language speaker, Water drum and horn rattles.

Speech to announce the songs

As mentioned before, there will be a speaker called Rarihowanahtha' (La-rih-hoe-wah-nah-ta) who will get up to speak. He will announce the lead singer and lead dancers of every song/dance and the name of the song/dance being sung. A House-keeper is also needed to conduct a social. He is called the Ratenonhsa'tsheristha,(La-deh-noo-za-steh-lee-sta) he makes sure the social is being conducted in the right way, and also determines who will sing or dance the next song. The speech to announce the song goes as follows:

Kenkio'kwa sewatonhon`siios kenikariwesha, ne:ne Rati'nonhsatstheristha'
Everyone listen for a little while the housekeeper

tahakeri:hon ahkerihowa'nathe ne:ne (singer's name) enshonkwaterennohthaseh
He gave permission to make an announcement (singer's name) he will sing for us

(name of song) nikarenno:ten tanon' o:ia (lead dancers name) nihohsenno:ten
The kind of song and also his name is (dancer's name)

ne enhanen:ri'ne ne kanon:nia ne o:nen skaia'takwe'ni:io o:nen enhontatewenen:ta'ne
He will lead the dance and now it is up to whenever they get prepared.

Eh Kati'niiotonhak ne Onkwa'nikonra.
So it is our understanding.

Tho.
Agreed.

Instruments used during social dance

Water drum- Kana'tsio:wi

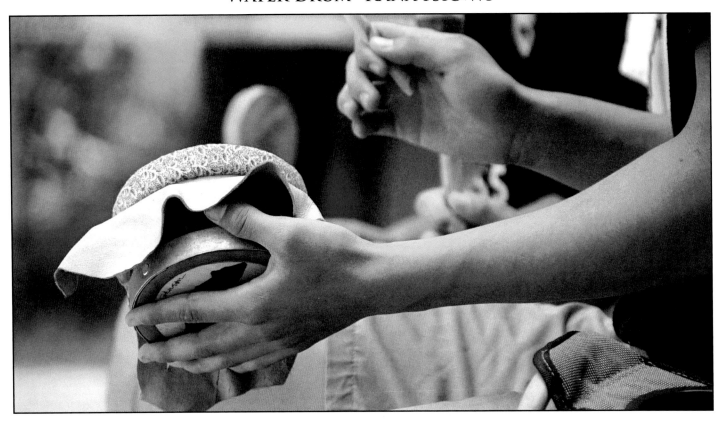

The water drum is very important and is considered a medicine. We use the water drum in socials and in ceremonies. The water drum is held by the lead singer of each of the songs and all the fellow singers follow that beat with their rattle. It is important for the people to respect the water drum along with every other instrument because of its importance and teachings. Without these things we cannot have the medicine of song in the way we have it now.

The drum is made of wood, which symbolizes the plant life, all the standing trees, medicines, as well as the food that sustains us. The leather is the hide of the deer, which symbolizes the animal life and how that also helps to provide food, clothing, and tools for the people. The water inside the drum is a necessity for all living people, plants, and animals. It represents all of the bodies of water that flow across the earth. The band that holds the drum together represents the life cycle. If you take one part of the drum away, it won't function properly. Just as the elements you see throughout nature. They all have a responsibility on this earth and without one of the elements, the rest could not function. Similar to the beat of the drum, the first sound you hear before you're born is the sound of your mother's heartbeat, and so this represents the heartbeat of our mother earth.

Horn Rattle- Ohstawa'

A long time ago the rattles we used to use were made out of elm bark. The elm bark was bent over a piece of wood made into a handle, so the bark can hold seeds to make the rattle sound. We used to also make rattles out of the ball of a gourd with seeds in it. After European contact our people utilized other materials and with this came the Horn Rattle. Our people started using bull horns and wood to create the rattles we use today.

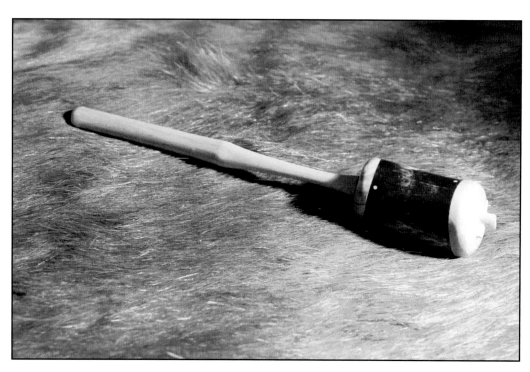

Voice- Owen:na

All of our music is used with singing with our voices. We use the rattles and drum to create the rhythm and we sing to create the song. Our music is different than the music you would hear on the radio, often times our music is just made up of different chants and sounds. We have a variety of different songs made up of these sounds and chants. The more familiar one becomes with the different chants one will be able to figure out which song is being sung without hearing the speaker tell you which song is being sung.

SONGS/DANCES

It is important that we have many social dances within our communities. We have our own songs and also some that have been adopted by other nations or tribes. Whatever the reason behind these songs and dances, they all serve a purpose and we do them with respect.

While we conduct these social dances, it is important that everything we do goes counterclockwise, such as dancing and passing out food. The reason we do everything in this direction is because this is the same direction that the earth revolves. In our culture we believe that is the way of life, creation and positivity. We do have dances that follow the other directions but those have their own time and normally deal with death. It is important to keep these things in mind and maintain that balance of good and bad. This stems back to the teachings of our creation story, with the left handed and right handed twins, which teach us harmony between the elements in creation and the negativity and positivity within ourselves.

Everything in our culture has a certain time and place for these songs or dances, and is to be respected. If we sing and dance at inappropriate times, the respect of those songs or instruments will be forgotten. That's how we start losing our ways. It is also important for the people to keep in mind that everyone that is able, should participate in the social. This is important because not everyone has the ability to get up and dance,

whether they are elderly, sick or whatever the reason may be, and we do it in honor and respect of them. Also because when these socials are being conducted, the environment influences positivity, and is a medicine. At times you will see someone who is unable to participate watching because this brings them joy. So we create that medicine for ourselves, for those unable to participate, and for all of creation.

It is also important for the people to keep in mind not to make fun of anyone for the way they dance or sing. When the humans were first created, each human being was given a different gift. Also, we must respect those people who are trying to learn because we are not born with this knowledge. We must be patient and share the knowledge with one another. When people begin to make fun of each other, or are being greedy with our songs, it removes the positivity out of the environment. The people are there to have a good time not to be the best or to show off, and if you are trying to do these things it's not the appropriate mindset for a social.

In this book we will mention how to do each social song and how to dance them. These teachings are based on the ways we do social dances here on the Mohawk Nation Territory of Akwesasne. We included as much songs and teachings as best we could but it must be kept in mind that because our culture stems from oral traditions, the history and meaning may be different to the different nations of the Haudenosaunee Confederacy. Each person will tell the meaning differently from the next. So, with that in mind, honoring the meaning behind the songs, how we conduct ourselves and having a good time is most important in doing these dances.

Stomp Dance/Standing Quiver- Watahtshero:ten

Standing Quiver is usually the first dance that is done at a social. It is a fairly easy dance, probably the easiest one out of all of them. This song is usually the first song because it is easy and is a good way to get all the people up to dance and everyone can join in the singing so it may lift their spirits.

The dance is like "follow the leader". Everyone follows the lead singer and stomps their feet in unison. The stomping of the feet is used as the beat to this song as there are no instruments used. The lead singer will chant and the rest of the singers/dancers will call back in response, according to each verse. The way this dance is organized male, female, male, female. The men will get up to dance first. After the men have made one full circle, then the women join in, in between the men.

The Standing Quiver dance came from a ceremony our people used to do, while still in our longhouse villages. Back in those days our people relied heavily on wild game. We had large hunting parties made up of the men of the community, to go out on hunting trips to gather meat for the community. We needed this food to survive throughout the winter. During this time, hunting was very dangerous and more risks were involved, since we didn't have the tools and resources we have today. Often times our men would get hurt and maybe even lose their life. Before these men would leave the village the community would gather all the hunters and their hunting tools. We would stand the quivers and other hunting tools in the middle of a field and we would dance around them to bring them good luck. While

we dance and sing around the quivers, the lead singer signals within the verse for everyone to face the center. This is the time that we send our good thoughts to the hunters, and their hunting tools. This is how we would show respect to the men because of all of the reasons stated before; they were risking themselves to sustain the community.

When these men returned they would also sing this song. It was their way to announce to the community that they were ready to come home. They would also sing this and stand all the quivers back in the middle and sometimes they would count the arrows to see how many were missing. This would indicate to them how many lives were lost. We would sing to honor the animal life that was sacrificed and show our respect to them as well. Today, we don't have the same risks as before and our community doesn't use these songs in the same way. However, it is used in our social dance out of respect to those hunters, because without them we wouldn't be a people today.

We also have the Cherokee Stomp Dance that we sometimes do at socials which require rattles and stomping of our feet to create the beat of the song. It is very similar to the Standing Quiver dance how it is a call and answer song.

The Cherokee Stomp Dance is a song that we traded with the Cherokee Nation. They use this song for ceremonies but we use this song in socials as a way to honor the friendship we had with these people. Since that Nation has given us these songs to use, we turned them into social songs as to not disturb the sanctity of those songs, but still respect them by singing these songs at socials. This is why it is important that we take our hats off during songs, dances and speeches because we must be respectful to those Nations and their ceremonies.

ROUND DANCE
TEIOKWATASE OR TSIOHTHWATASE:THA

The Round Dance is a slow song. The way this is danced is the same male, female, male, female pattern. All the dancers make a circle around the singers, while holding hands. The dance should follow the beat of the drum. The dance will start going counterclockwise and be lead with your right foot. Half way though the song, the lead singer will give a signal to the dancers to change the direction. They will then dance clockwise, and lead with their left-foot.

This dance was not originally our song; it was adopted from Western Nations of the Plains. However, our people use it and relate it to our culture and people. As stated before everything in our culture relates back to the creation story to the right handed and left handed twins that created all of life. All of things that represent life and positivity, move in the counter clockwise direction because this is the direction that the earth rotates. All things that deal with death and/or negativity, move in the clockwise direction, because this is the opposite direction of the earth's rotation. The round dance is the only dance that we will dance in both directions. The reason for this is that it symbolizes our life. How we must respect and acknowledge the balance of good and bad. Such as, all of the struggles of our lives, the blessings, and how with new life comes death. It is a reminder for our people to live in a good mind and peace among our people. Every person makes mistakes, and also does good things in life and we must not dwell on the negative aspects of a person, or of ourselves. We must live in unity and peace among man and woman, child and elder, Native or non-native, human or animal, etc. We must respect the different aspects of life which the creator has given us. He made us all different for a reason and we must honor our teachings and give thanks and acknowledgement to both negative and positive. Our people understood this and that's why they were able to use this song and relate it to our culture.

Fish Dance- Kentsionhneha

The Fish dance is a fast dance. To dance to this song, is to follow the beat of the drum. In this dance, the basic steps are one-two step. However, each person develops their own style with his or her own expression of their movements. We start the dance, again with the men. Each man picks a male partner, and dance in a single file line with one partner in front of the other. The partners are always supposed to face one another, so the person in front will be dancing backwards while the other partner dances forward. When the lead singer changes the beat, it is a signal to the partners to switch places. After the men have made one full circle, the women will find a partner, then join the line in between the male partners. Then the male dancing backwards will be partners with the woman partner who is in front. The second female partner will then dance backwards and will become partners with the second male partner.

This dance is an original song of our people. A long time ago when we lived in our longhouse villages, our people were very connected to the natural world. We had vast traditional ecological knowledge that allowed us to understand the cycles of the land, and beings within nature, one of those things being the fish. Our people would fish during winter and summer. In the spring, they noticed how the fish would spawn. They would see these fish facing each other while moving in circles, and so during our dance we imitate the movements of the fish. We had a lot of respect for the fish life and its sacrifice to sustain us, and so we acknowledge them with this dance.

Duck Dance- Sorah'neha

The duck dance is a really fun dance. This dance originates from when our hunters would hunt for ducks. If you ever seen a duck before it takes off from the water you will notice that it doesn't fly straight up into the sky, it flies along the surface of the water before it finally takes off. A long time ago, our hunting methods were to take our canoes into the rivers and hold up big nets. They would have one man scare the ducks so they would take off. The ducks would take off straight into the nets.

This dance is another imitation of the actions of the ducks. The men represent the hunters holding their nets, and the women representing the ducks. The men will dance first, finding a partner and dancing side by side. After the men have gone around in a full circle, then the women will find a partner and face the line of men.

The women dance backwards while the men face dancing forward. The footwork of this dance is similar to the stomp dance, stomping their feet in unison to the beat. The lead singer will change the beat of the song to signal that the men put their arms up as if they are holding a net with their partner. Then the women will lock arms and run under their arms, as if they were ducks trying to take off. When the beat changes back again, the men quickly put their arms down to "catch" the ducks. Some women will get caught in between the pairs of men as if they were caught. This song is a favorite among children and young people, because many people will get silly. In between verses some will even mimic the sounds of the duck and flap their arms like wings.

OLD MOCCASIN- ATAKWAKA:ION

Old moccasin is similar to Fish Dance, the only difference is each partner faces forward. The footwork and pace is the same as fish dance. The men start the dance and after the men have made a full circle, the women then come in to dance. This is another dance which each person dances differently. Each person has a style they've developed of their own and expresses their enjoyment of life and the dance.

This dance originates from an old ceremony we used to have for the apples. Along time ago when the apples were ripe, we would have a ceremony. It was to celebrate and give respect for our good harvest during the fall months. To express our appreciation for our harvest, two elders, one male and one female would be selected for this ceremony. The two best moccasin makers of the whole village would make two pairs of moccasins for a male and a female. Then these moccasins were given to the two elders to choose who would be best to give them to. So they would observe the young ones who are participating and think about the way they would conduct themselves within the community. These elders would watch them all while they danced and would find one that stood out to them. This would excite the young ones to dance hard and use their fanciest moves. The elders would look for the best dancers, not for their moves but for how much they show their respect and appreciation for the natural world.

When we would do these ceremonies, other dancers would see the pair with the beautiful moccasins and would let them lead the dance. This was a sign of respect because they knew that the male and female were chosen for being respectful. Over time, our people lost the meaning of this ceremony and it remains today as the Old Moccasin dance.

FRIENDSHIP DANCE- ATERO'SERAHNEHA

The Friendship dance is a slow dance, and it's pretty easy to do. It is a partner dance between men and women. The footwork to this dance is a two-step dance. The dancers will bring one foot forward and bring it back, then the other foot forward and then back. They repeat these steps in unison with their partners. Then the lead singers will signal to the dancers with a change of the beat, for them to face each other. When the beat changes back to its normal beat the dancers will then face forward again.

It is said that this was not one of our original songs but came to be used by our people because this dance was done anytime the different Nations came together for Political gatherings. It was a way of declaring peace and friendship among the nations outside of our territories and outside of the confederacy. It also reinforces positive relationships.

WOMAN'S DANCE- TSIONATONWISEN'NEHA

The Women's Dance is one of the most important dances. It must always be sung and danced at all socials. Our people live in a matrilineal society. We hold women with high respect because it was a woman, the Sky Woman who started the process of all creation. Our people know women hold that gift to give life and the reason we are all living. Women play a really big role in the way we govern ourselves. A long time ago, our men would go out hunting and would leave the village. It was the women who would watch over the village, take care of the young, and sustain them. So, whenever it came a time to pick a leader/chief the women would be the ones to appoint the leadership. Women were also in charge of naming all the children, arranging marriages, and taking care of the gardens.

This song is important because it is an acknowledgement to all the women who sustain us, and especially to our mother, the Earth who sustains all life on her. We recognize that both men and women have their different responsibilities as Onkwehon:we (the Original Human beings) to protect and take care of Mother Earth and to maintain the balance so carrying of female respon- our ceremonies may continue to be out. We have a deep understanding of the relationship between male and and how it coexists. One of the sibilities of men is to sing these songs for the women.

In our creation story, it was a woman whom we call Sky Woman who created the earth. In short version, she fell from the Sky World from a hole she dug under the Tree of Life, while digging for roots. As she was digging, seeds and roots got stuck under her nails. She dug too far and created a hole that she fell through. As she was falling she tried to grab the earth and the roots taking hold of more seeds. Descending from the Sky world she fell through darkness down towards the world. Before she created it, the world was made up of all water, and contained only a giant turtle, water animals and birds. A flock of geese noticed that she was falling and helped her land safely onto the turtle's back. The water animals came to aid her in whatever she needed and so she requested soil. All the water animals realized there was soil at the very bottom of the water but it was very far. All animals took their turns to retrieve the soil and failed. Until the muskrat took his turn, he held his breath as long as he could. He was determined to get the soil for her. Unfortunately, the muskrat died and floated back to the surface of the water with the soil in his little paw. The Sky Woman acknowledge the great sacrifice the Muskrat made for her and she spread the soil around the turtle's back while singing our sacred seed songs and dancing the Women's Shuffle. The seeds fell from her hands and nails and the earth was created.

This dance is just for the women. All the women will get up and dance in a single file line. Women will wait for a full verse before getting up to dance. This is because the first verse is in respect for the Sky Woman. Women imitate the same dance that the Sky Woman danced to create the earth. When Women dance you will see their feet barely lift off of the ground. They shuffle their feet against the earth as if to massage the turtle's back with their feet. In this dance, the eldest women are supposed to be at the front to set the pace of the dance. If the fastest dancers go in front, there will be a gap in between the women as they dance. Women often weave inward and outward to represent planting and our vines of the squash and beans. It is also a good dance to strengthen the women's hips for childbirth.

The men sing these songs for the women in the best way they can, it is the men's time to express themselves to the women through songs. The men will watch the women dance to show their admiration and respect. This dance is a favorite among a lot of people because of how beautiful it can be.

Alligator Dance-Tekanionton'neha

This dance was traded with our people from the Seminole people. It is similar to how the Haudenosaunee hold certain animals, like the eagle in high regards. The Seminoles honor the alligators. This dance was given to our people as an exchange for certain medicines that were given to a Seminole man who fell ill while in Haudenosaunee territory. The Seminole people were very grateful for helping one of their own. So, a friendship was created between our people and the Seminoles. It was given to us to protect us if we were to travel south to Seminole territory.

This song is a partner dance between male and female. It is the women who ask the men to dance. When a woman has found a partner they will lock arms while dancing. One man and woman will lead the dance, and the other pairs will line up behind them. The men will dance on the inside of the circle, and the women on the outside. The man represents the head of the alligator, and the woman represents the tail.

Some of the verses are interactive with the dancers, such as one verse can be call-and-answer, and another will signal the dancers to stomp their feet. Also, the lead singer will change the beat of the drum to signal to the dancers to spin in a circle. The man will spin in place with his arm still locked with the woman as if she were his tail. This symbolizes when the alligator spins in the water and how they whip their tails to attract mates.

Shake the Bush or Naked Dance- Ononsta'keha

The Shake the Bush Dance or also known as the Naked Dance is a hard dance to do, but once the people get the hang of the steps, it can be a lot of fun. It requires 4 people to dance together and begins with the women dancing. The women will form a circle around the men singers and will assist with singing the first five introductory songs. The introductory songs are a little slower than the rest of the songs. The men will start the songs, and when there is a change of tone, the women will help sing the middle part and together the women and men finish the song. Then the dancing starts. The women will get in a group of four. They have their partner at their side and two will face forward while two other women will face them, dancing backwards. The footwork of this dance is like your kicking towards the dancer across from you, but the dancers kick in unison with the beat and with each other. The dancers will kick with opposite legs so they will not hit each other. Your feet will skim the floor as you kick, like you are clearing bushes.

Sometimes it is very hard to get the hang of this dance but once you do everyone is laughing and having a good time. Then once the dance gets much faster, the men will join in. The men will get in a group of four as well and get in between the women. So the two women dancing backwards will face one pair of men, while the other pair of men will dance backwards to face the women dancing forward. When the singers change the beat of the drum, it signals to the dancers to switch places, so whoever is facing backwards will be facing forward and vice versa.

This song originates from the Sioux people of the west. They call this song the Shake the Bush Dance because in the summer when the berries were ripe, the women would go to the berry bushes and put a basket on the ground under the bush. Then they would lift their skirts to their knees and kick the bush so the berries would fall into the basket or into their skirt. So this dance imitates those movements that those women made to gather the berries. However, some people also say that when the Sioux and our tribe met, the Mohawk people have a very "tongue in cheek" humor so when they noticed that when the men would do strenuous work, they would take off all of their outer layers of clothing so they were almost naked, and so the Mohawks started calling them, Ronatehnontston:ni, or "the Naked People." So this name stuck to this song when it was traded with our people and that is why we call it the Naked Dance as well as Shake the Bush.

SMOKE DANCE-OTSHATA'NEHA

Some say that the origin of Smoke Dance stems from our Thunder Ceremony. The evolution of Smoke Dance has adapted into a competition dance over the years when Pow Wows first began to start. Some verses of the Smoke dance start out very slow, then get very fast.

Some people of the Haudenosaunee believe that it has stemmed from the Thunder Ceremony, because the slow verses resemble how we do the Thunder Dance. Only the men dance the slower verses, but they will dance like they are reenacting scenes from war or from hunting. It is meant to show the people the bravery that is required to do either of those things. They will draw invisible bows, or even carry a club with them while they dance. Then the beat becomes fast, the footwork stays on beat with the drum and time their movements with the jump beats or also known as trick beats. Each dancer has their own style of dancing because dancers learn to express themselves in their arm movements or their footwork. For competition dancing, the main rule is to stay on beat with the drum. Since it is so fast, it can be difficult and this is why they have this for competitions. It is very fun to dance once you get the footwork down and familiarize yourself with the songs. It is also very fun to watch because the female dancers move so gracefully and the male dancers are very animated.

ROBIN DANCE- TSISKOKO'NEHA

The Robin Dance is one of our original songs. To dance this people need a lead singer, an assistant, and rattles. The lead singers will stand facing one another and everyone will line up sideways, behind the two singers. The pattern is male, female, female, male. Everybody dances a side-step to the beat of the rattles. In the middle of the verse the lead singers will give a signal for all the dancers to make a complete turn until they are facing away from the person in front of them. Some people will do a little hop to face forward or to face backwards. This represents the movement of the Robin in the springtime when they are looking for food for their babies. The Robin will hop in place to turn in different directions. This dance is to honor the bird life which keeps humans entertained by their music. The Robin also plays an important role in the creation story and was given a duty to the humans to tell them when it is time for spring. When we see the Robin we honor him for his message and the coming of a new season.

Fishing or Canoe Dance- Iontahrio:tha

The Fishing or Canoe Dance is a fun dance. Just like Shake the Bush Dance, at the beginning of this dance the women will circle up and help sing the introduction verses. The introductory songs are a little slower than the rest of the songs. The men will start the songs, and when there is a change of tone, the women will help sing the middle part and together the women and men finish the song. Then beat of the song will become faster, that is when the dancing starts.

The women will do the women's shuffle in an inner circle around the singers, and then the men will do a stomp dance in a circle around the women. In the middle of the song the lead singer will chant like how we do in stomp dance. He'll say "Ioh, Ioh." The rest of the singers will respond with, "Wa-he" This signals the men to tap on the shoulders of the women or pull them into their circle. So when all the women have been pulled into their circle someone will shout and all the dancers respond with, "Weeeee." This tells all the women to go back into their inner circle. This goes on for at least seven verses, for the last verse turns into a stomp dance song. All the men and women will join into one circle and finish it in this way.

What needs to be remembered for this song is that we all need to conduct ourselves in a respectful way. When the men "pull" or tap on the women it is not in a rough manner, or inappropriate way. Also, the women must conduct themselves respectfully. This song is meant to honor the fish life and be a song to show our respect and acknowledgement to the fishermen. The Men represent the Fisherman in their canoes, and the women are the fish swimming downstream. When the men tap on the women, it is like they captured the fish in their nets. Back in the time when our people still lived in Longhouse villages, being a good fisherman or hunter was an honorable role to be in. They were ensuring the survival of our communities and so we show our respect with our many songs and dances that are meant to bless our hunters and fishers, or give them good luck. So, we must remember this when we are doing this dance, and that we must conduct ourselves in a respectful way.

Sharpened Stick Dance – Ahonte'nio'thi:iate

The Sharpened Stick dance or Sharpen the Stick dance is a faster song. It is similar to the way that we dance Fish dance or the Old Moccasin dance. It is a one-two step that changes with each dancer. Each dancer has their own style of dancing because it is an expressive dance. This dance starts out with the men, like most of our social songs. The men will find a partner and will line up in a single file line. Then when the first verse is over, the women will join in with a partner. The two women will get between the pair of men so it is in order man, woman, woman, man. When the beat changes, this signals for the dancers to trade places with the person in front of them, so now the two men are in between the two women.

Some say that the meaning behind this song comes from the planting time when we would begin putting the seeds in the ground. The men would make sharpened sticks to poke holes in the ground for the seeds to go in. Others say that this song is meant to remind the men and young boys to keep their minds sharp. Since our culture is based from oral traditions some of the meanings of our songs and dances have been lost or changes with time and so there can be many different interpretations behind one song.

Raccoon Dance- Atironhnehac

The Raccoon Dance is very fun. You don't know how long a verse will last because it is up to the lead dancer to end a verse. You have to be prepared to dance long or sometimes only a short while. The head of the house will pick one lead dancer and a lead singer. The lead dancer dances in the front of the line and the rest of the dancers will line behind them. However, only the men will get up to start the dance. The introductory verses are slower than the rest of the song. This is when the men will dance very slow and sometimes will slouch their backs like raccoons. Then when the beat of the drum becomes faster, that signals the women can to the dance, in pairs. The order of the dance is man, woman, woman, and man. Each verse starts out with a steady beat then will become faster and faster until the lead dancer shouts or shrieks, that signals to the lead singer to change the verse. It is up to the lead dancer how long the verse will go. The longer the lead dancer waits to shriek, the faster the beat of the drum. In the middle of the verses, there is a change of tone which also signals for the dancers to switch places with their partners. This song is really fun and is very unpredictable just like the raccoon.

Passenger Pigeon- Orite'neha

A long time ago when the people still lived in our longhouse villages, the winters were much harsher than they are today. Our people would eat dried meats and different foods throughout the cold winter season. There is not as much wild game to hunt during this time, so the people would often crave the taste of all the various wild game animals. As the winter began to change to spring, different birds would migrate back to our territory. One of these birds was the Passenger Pigeon, which were very large birds similar to the wild turkeys that we hunt today. They say that they were much easier to hunt. Since they were not afraid of humans, you could walk right up to them. The people began hunting the Passenger Pidgeon because they were so easy to hunt. Then our people began over hunting this bird so much that the bird actually went extinct. This song that we sing is to honor the Passenger Pigeon for its sacrifice that it gave to us so it may provide for us. It is also to honor them because our people forgot to show respect by not hunting too much. In some communities this dance is used for a ceremony. We must find a reciprocal balance by giving thanks for what we take from nature.

This is a dance that only requires using horn rattles and the stomping of the feet. The men get up first and form two lines. After the first song, the men will begin moving forward in a marching motion, while stomping their feet to make the beat. After two or three songs the women will join in between the men. The lead singer or singers will change the tone of their voice to signal in each song, for the dancers to turn in towards each other. Then they will return marching forward.

Rabbit Dance- Tehahontaneken'neha

The Rabbit Dance originates from a legend that our people have known for hundreds of years. A long time ago, a young boy and a young girl wandered into the forest near their village. There they saw a rabbit that came very close to them. To their amazement the rabbit spoke to them. The rabbit asked them to follow him and that he had a gift that he wanted them to bring back to their people. So, the boy and the girl followed the rabbit deep into the forest, until they came across a village of rabbits. There were hundreds of rabbits gathered there. There were all kinds of different rabbits, different sizes, and colors. The rabbit they first met told the boy and the girl that they cannot enter the village, but they can watch and learn. The whole village of rabbits began to sing and dance. Just like the humans did. The rabbits began to partner up, male and female, and joining hands. The boy and the girl observed the way their hands swayed, and their footwork how they went two steps forward and one step back. The boy and the girl couldn't help but smile. After the dance was finished the rabbit told the boy and the girl to bring that song and dance back to their village. It was the Rabbit's gift and reminder to the humans to enjoy each other no matter how different we may be. Then, the boy and the girl ran back to their village and told the people of their experience. The adults in the community listened with doubtful smirks on their faces. They did not believe the children. The children persisted saying that the adults should go see it for themselves. The adults decided to send an elder who was much

respected, to satisfy the children's wishes. The boy and the girl led the elder to the spot they have seen the rabbits dance. That is when the elder seen all the rabbits. He saw how different all the rabbits were, and noticed the way that they all dance. Once he saw what the children had seen, he was very happy. The elder returned to the village with the children and told the people of his experience. Finally, all the people believed the children and started to learn the Rabbit dance.

The Rabbit Dance is a couple's dance. A woman will pick a man to be their partner for this dance. It is said that the men are not supposed to say no to a woman if he is asked, because it is disrespectful. It is considered an honor to be asked to dance by a woman and so men should be respectful and dance. Some say if the man refuses to dance with the woman, they must give the woman $5! This is humor that has developed over the years at socials as to remind the men that they should never say no to a woman's request. This dance is fairly slow. The two partners join hands while facing each other, but when they join hands both partners will have their arms crossed while holding hands. To start the dance, the couple will start swaying their hands, once forward, once back and then in a full circle. The footwork pattern is two steps forward, and one step back. They do this in unison with the swaying of their joined hands, and in unison with the beat of the drum. Sometimes it can be difficult to get the hang of it at first, but once you understand the motions, it becomes easier.

During the song, the lead singer will change the beat of the drum. This is a signal for the dancers to slowly turn in a full circle.

We continue to do this dance because it teaches us many important lessons. This dance has taught us to appreciate each other and enjoy each other no matter how different we may be from others. It teaches us that in life we may take two steps forward but then fall back one step, but it's important to remember to keep going. It also teaches us that every person in our community has a voice and deserves to be heard, especially our children. Even though they are little they still have a lot to teach us.

The Mosquito Dance- Kariahta'neha

The Mosquito Dance is a dance that is borrowed from the Choctaw Nation of the State of Mississippi. It came to Akwesasne, when a Mohawk man married a woman of the Choctaw Nation. The Mohawk Nation and the other Haudenosaunee communities have accepted this song as a part of our social dances. This song is a couple's dance between male and female. The couples will hold each other's little fingers with the same side hand so that they are facing opposite directions. Then they will kick in the opposite direction. In the middle of the verse, the lead singer will signal to the dancers to make a complete turn while still kicking. Before the couples turn, they will give out a yell. Once they complete their circle they continue dancing. In Akwesasne we use a water drum and horn rattles as our instruments but in Mississippi they use two sticks that they hit together to make the beat of the drum.

This song is not often sung here in Akwesasne but it is still considered a part of our collection of social songs and dances.

Gartered Dance- Atsihna'neha

The Gartered Dance acknowledges the garter that men wear around their legs. The garter denotes protection for our hunters and men from physical and spiritual dangers. The garter holds on their legs, deer toes which rattle and scare off bad spirits and physical harm. The Deer toe is used because it is the deer's first defense. In many of our dances, ceremony or socials, the men will dance in an outer circle with the women and children in the center. This represents a circle the men from around them that they will protect and provide for them.

The Gartered Dance is similar to the Standing Quiver Dance, but it requires more movement when the beat changes. It starts with a lead singer and an assistant. The dancers will get in a single file line behind the lead singers with two men in front and two women as their partners in between the men. So the pattern will be male, female, male, female. It is a side-step stomp dance style. There are three beat changes. When the first beat changes, this signals for the dancers to face their partners. At the second beat change, the partners change places. When the third beat changes this signal indicates for the partners to change places again so they are in their original places.

The Cold Dance or Dance of the North- Othore'keha

This song translated into English means "the dance of the North", the Cold Dance, or sometimes called the "Eskimo Dance". This song arrived to our people around 50 years ago when a Mohawk chief had brought it back after a visit to Quebec. This song is characterized as being unusually long and the musical form is slightly complicated for new singers to learn.

For this song, the footwork is a tricky two step almost like the footwork of the Fish Dance. The dancers will dance in two single file lines with the men on the inside and their female partners to the right of them.

This song is not often sung here in Akwesasne but it is still considered a part of our collection of social songs and dances.

THE CHICKEN DANCE- KITKIT'NEHA

The Chicken dance is not one of our original songs it comes from one of the Western Nations we have come into contact with a long time ago. This song was adopted by the Seneca Nation then spread to the other nations of the Haudenosaunee Territory. However, the Seneca Nation territory is in close proximity to the Shawnee, Osage, and Cherokee Nation territories. So, the exact root of where this dance comes from and its meaning is not very certain. The Cherokee, the Shawnee and even the tribes from Alberta all have their own ceremony style of Chicken Dance. This song could have been adopted by any of these tribes. Some say that this dance is a fertility dance, and is meant to bless the men and women who dance it. This song is also danced during Pow Wows, and the dancers can be seen wearing lots of feathers that resemble a rooster.

To dance this dance it is quite similar to the Old Moccasin dance with Fish Dance style of footwork. The pattern of dancers is male, female, female, male. When the beat changes, this signals for the dancers to change places with the person behind them or in front of them. So, then the pattern should then be female, male, male, female. Then the beat changes a second time and this is when they change places again. At the very end of the song the lead dancer will crow loudly like a rooster. This song is not often sung here in Akwesasne but it is still considered a part of our collection of social songs and dances.

DELAWARE SKIN DANCE/STICK DANCE- KAHNEWA:IEN

This song comes from the Delaware people, which were once Algonkian language speakers and now they are called Anishinabek. The Delaware people were once warriors for Joseph Brant during the American Revolution. After the war, in 1784 they brought their families to safety to the Grand River territory in Six Nations. They had their own street that then became Delaware road, because they once had a big house there which they conducted their ceremonies. During this time, the Six Nations longhouses adopted their Skin Dance as a social dance. We show our friendship and respect to those Delaware or Anishinabek people through the use of their song in socials. So, when these songs are being sung or dance at a social it is important that we show our respect to that Nation and their ceremonies by taking off our hats and conducting ourselves in a good way, as not to disturb the sanctity of those ceremonies.

The ceremony which the Stick Dance has stemmed from similarly imitates their Skin Dance Ceremony. Where they stretch the hide between two men and hit the hide with sticks. When our people adopted the song, it evolved into sitting on the bench and using sticks to hit the bench. So, the horn rattles or the water drum is not needed for this song.

The footwork of this dance is similar to the Fish dance or the Old Moccasin dance. Some verses are very slow and some are very fast. It starts with the men making a single file line, and the lead dancer in the front. The men will make one full circle before the women join in. The women will make a single file line, side by side with the men's line. The women will dance on the inside and the men on the outside of the circle.

It is very popular among the younger people who still have a lot of energy because this song is one of the fastest social songs. It is usually carried out at the very end of the social.

It must be kept in mind again that some of the meanings of our songs may be interpreted differently by different people, or different Nations of the Confederacy. Our oral tradition style of teachings makes it ever more challenging to search for the true meaning and history behind why we do these songs and dances and where they came from. A few of these songs do not include its origins or meanings, because their meaning has either been lost or has not been tracked down yet. It is for these reasons, that we are recording the stories, dances and songs so that it may never be lost.

Many of these songs and dances we do at socials today have been adopted, gifted or traded with other nations that we once came into contact with. We continue to do these dances so we can honor the friendship we have with those nations. We also continue to express our thankfulness for all of creation through song and dance.

Not everyone starts out as the best dancers or singers. It takes time, practice and participating in socials to fully understand. We encourage all people to attend socials around your community and educate yourself in the meanings and history of our songs. Don't be afraid to use your gifts and don't forget to have fun.

DEDICATION

It is as one mind that we give thanks to all the elders and all the people who helped us in our gathering of knowledge and history. Especially, to the original writers of the first Social Dance book such as Tom Porter, Mike McDonald, Barbara Barnes, and all the past NNATC Cultural Educators for their contributions to this new book. This was no easy task to hunt for knowledge. Without all the help of the people in our community and outside communities, we wouldn't have been able to spread these teachings to our people. A special thanks to our current NNATC Cultural Educators, including Donovan Thompson, Shatekaronhioton Fox and Karahkwino-Tina Square for their hard work and efforts to make this book complete.

Our songs and our dances carry our people through these changing times and remind us all the true meaning behind being an Onkwehon:we (Original Human Being). Singing and Dancing is a medicine and is one of the many forms of expressing our thankfulness for all of creation, which is the basis of our ways of life. We acknowledge the long line of people who still today continue to carry on our traditions and ways of life, so that it may pass on to the next seven generations.

With Kanikonhri:io (good mind), Kasatstentshe':rah (power) and Sken:nen (peace), we carry on our original teachings, our roles and responsibilities as it should be. We let our elders rest assured that they have fulfilled their duties. It is our turn as the future generations to carry the burden and continue the duties the Creator has assigned us as Onkwehon:we people.

Nia:wen kowa.

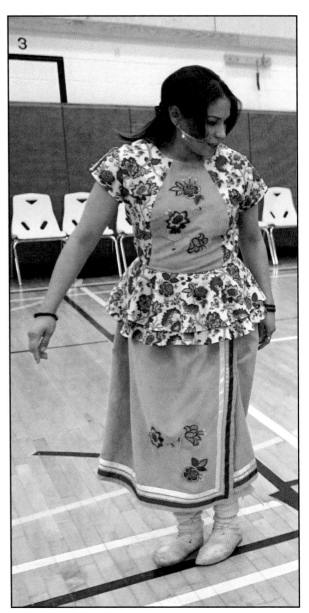

The Native North American Travelling College has been at the forefront of cultural education and revitalization. It was established on the Akwesasne Mohawk Territory in 1974 under the name North American Indian Travelling College by Ernest Kaientaronkwen Benedict and Michael Kanentakeron Mitchell.

The Native North American Travelling College continues to evolve to meet the needs of a changing community. We need more than ever to promote and preserve our language culture and history, not only for our own sake, but to foster a greater appreciation and understanding in the outside community.

1 Ronathahon:ni Lane
Akwesasne, Ontario K6H 5R7

Tele: 613 932-9452
Fax: 613 932-0092
web: www.nnatc.org

P.O. Box 273
Hogansburg, NY 13655